MILESTONES OF THOUGHT

W9-BVY-859

LUDWIG FEUERBACH

THE ESSENCE OF CHRISTIANITY

Edited and abridged by
E. GRAHAM WARING
Lawrence College
and
F. W. STROTHMANN
Stanford University

FREDERICK UNGAR PUBLISHING CO.
NEW YORK

MILESTONES
OF THOUGHT
in the History of Ideas

General Editor
F. W. STROTHMANN
Stanford University

Fourth Printing, 1973

Copyright 1957 by
Frederick Ungar Publishing Co.

Printed in the United States of America

Library of Congress Catalog Card Number: 57-8650

ISBN 0-8044-6145-7

INTRODUCTION

Ludwig Feuerbach
[1804-1872]

"Then came Feuerbach's *Essence of Christianity*. . . .
One must himself have experienced the liberating effect of
this book to get an idea of it. Enthusiasm was general; we
all became at once Feuerbachians." [1] While the "enthusiasm" of Engels and Marx was later to be tempered by
criticism, they were to repeat the basic elements of his
analysis of religion with little change in what has become
the most influential attack on religion in the modern world.
Feuerbach's formulation, therefore, is truly a living issue
in the problem of the interpretation of religion.

The facts of Feuerbach's life which are relevant for an
understanding of the present work can be simply recounted.
He was born in 1804, in Landshut, Bavaria, the son of an
eminent jurist, Paul Johann Anselm Feuerbach. He was
about twenty when he entered Heidelberg to study
theology, intending a career within the church. Through the
influence of a professor, he was attracted to the thought
of Hegel; soon he went to Berlin, where for two years he embraced the Hegelian philosophy. After a brief period of
scientific study, he launched his teaching career as
Privatdozent at Erlangen; an attack on the idea of personal
immortality in "Thoughts on Death and Immortality" made
advancement, however, impossible. In 1837 he married,
and for most of the rest of his life he lived at Bruckberg,
supported chiefly by his wife's investments. The present
work was published in 1841, and established Feuerbach as

[1] Frederick Engels, *Ludwig Feuerbach and the Outcome of Classical
German Philosophy* (New York: International Publishers, 1941), p. 18.

a leader among the radical left-wing Hegelians. Although he sympathized with the revolutionary movements of 1848, he took no active part in them; his role remained that of a teacher and essayist. His influence depended principally upon the present work, which was translated into English, French, and Russian; his later works were less enthusiastically received. By the time of his death in 1872, his direct influence had waned considerably.

Properly to understand the present work, we must set it over against the background of the intellectual situation out of which it grew. Feuerbach claimed to have made a fresh start in philosophy, a start for which he owed nothing to the "speculations" of previous thinkers. But though he does, indeed, represent a radical divergence, he is clearly a child of his times.

The central issue of philosophy as it developed in the seventeenth and eighteenth centuries was the problem of knowledge. The truth of ideas was increasingly investigated by an analysis of their sources. In the extreme empiricism of David Hume, all ideas were tested in terms of the sense impressions regarded as their ultimate basis. The claim to religious knowledge, like the claim to scientific knowledge, must support itself by appeal to experiential—for Hume, sensory—data. In effect this standpoint meant that the idea of God had to be justified—if it could be justified—as an inference. In his *Dialogues Concerning Natural Religion,* Hume showed clearly how weak the probability of the existence of God is, when the idea is regarded as an inference from sense data regarded as "effects."

In Immanuel Kant, the attacks of the Enlightenment on religious ideas culminate; at the same time "the problem of religion," like the problem of knowledge, receives a new formulation. Kant accepts Hume's criticisms of the idea of God, conceived as an idea about the world of existence; indeed, his analyses of the traditional "arguments" for the existence of God are more systematic and thoroughgoing than Hume's. But knowledge of the universe in which we live—of which science represents the most detailed and precise formulation—does not represent the whole of man's response to the real. In addition to the response we call Science, there is the response of esthetic and moral value judgments. Ideas which are inappropriate to the "theoretical" sphere of Science may be necessary for the "practical" area of ethics. For Kant, the idea of God is such an idea. Rejected from the sum total of concepts proper to knowledge of the physical world, it returns as a basic affirmation and presupposition of the moral life. Man being what he is, it is an inevitable idea of the practical reason.

Within orthodox Protestant theology, on the other hand, there had been a constant tendency, for a multiplicity of reasons, to emphasize the idea of divine transcendence; to maintain that God is a God radically other than the world, touching the world chiefly through miraculously breaking-into the rule of natural law.

Both the philosophic and the religious modes of thought shaped the situation in which the philosophy of Hegel was developed. Hegel's system sought to be all-embracing, to provide an ultimate explanation and justification of all the diverse ways in which man has conceived his relation to the world. The instrument by means of which this attempt was made was "dialectic."

The Hegelian use of this term is easier to illustrate than to define. Its significance can be seen from a glance at the history of philosophy. If idealism, a philosophy built on the significant factor of thought in human experience, becomes dominant, we may call such an idealism the *thesis* of a dialectical movement. What idealism denies, however, is as significant as what it asserts; idealism represents only a partial grasp of human experience; its denials and omissions call forth a protesting philosophy, perhaps a form of materialism, which is the *antithesis*. The "thesis" and its "antithesis" present an impasse, unless their seemingly contradictory truths can be creatively fused in a higher *Synthesis*. Hegel saw this dialectical movement from thesis to antithesis to synthesis as the very structure not merely of thought, but also of reality. For him, all the ways in which man had sought to interpret his place in the world—of which religion is a significant one—represent not only the unfolding of *man's* thought but also the unfolding of the "Idea," i.e., of the nature of being itself. In Hegel's own "synthesis," religion and philosophy are seen as two ways of responding to the "Idea" which, though differing in form (concrete imagery versus abstract concepts), have a common content of knowledge.

Hegel's followers—and Feuerbach was one of them—divided sharply in the way in which they appropriated his insights. We can see this divergence in respect to the problem of religion. The "right-wing" Hegelians, under attack by representatives of orthodoxy, stressed the oneness of truth-content in religion and philosophy. The "left-wing" Hegelians, with whom Feuerbach was associated, concentrated on the incompatibility of orthodoxy and philosophy.

The attack on religion by the left-wing Hegelians was made prominent by the publication of David Strauss' *Leben Jesu* in 1835. (Like the present work, it was translated into English by the novelist George Eliot.) In this work, Strauss sought to account historically for the ideas of the Christian faith by treating the gospels as folk myths expressing the aspirations of the Jewish people. It is important to see how Feuerbach advances beyond Strauss. By analyzing the origin of religion psychologically rather than historically, Feuerbach seeks in principle to account for all religion, not just Christianity. And by showing that religion arises from genuine human need, and therefore makes a positive contribution to life, he avoids Strauss' onesidedness.

Feuerbach's main thesis may be stated simply. Religion arises from the needs, wishes, and lacks of human life. Religious ideas embody emotional attitudes and real insights into what Man ought to be which are expressed in fitting imagery, projected into the extramental world, and objectified. Statements about God are then regarded as truths about extramundane existence; in truth, they are about man himself.

Space prohibits an examination of this thesis in detail. But we must note its impact, and the use to which it was put by later thinkers. Engels' remark about the "liberating" effect of the book has already been cited. Similar was the response of Wagner, who saw in Feuerbach "the ideal exponent of the radical release of the individual." [2] Marx termed Feuerbach a second Luther in the history of man's emancipation from illusion. This kind of response should not be surprising; the work was intended to be a contribution to man's understanding of himself; Feuerbach had originally intended its title to be the Greek motto "Know Thyself."

Certainly Marx's acceptance of Feuerbach's main contention constitutes the book's principal historical influence. This acceptance is not unqualified. He terms Feuerbach's mode of thought too abstract and speculative; he objects that Feuerbach deals inadequately with the social determination of the "projected" religious ideas. But the main Feuerbachian position remains intact. Marx pays him the tribute: "His work consists in the dissolution of the religious world into its secular basis. . . . Feuerbach resolves the religious essence into the human." [3]

But Marx goes beyond Feuerbach. For Feuerbach, man projects his nature, and then worships that nature objectified as a lawgiver, as God. For Marx, it is not Feuerbach's "man" which does the projecting, but society and State; their "projections," i.e., their legal and moral systems, can be traced to economic modes of production. [4] Both Marx's indebtedness to Feuerbach and his advance beyond him are expressed in the following passage:

[2] Richard Wagner, *My Life* (New York: Dodd, Mead, 1911), Vol. I, p. 522.
[3] Karl Marx, "Theses on Feuerbach," in Engels, *op. cit.*, p. 83.
[4] Cf. Sidney Hook, *From Hegel to Marx* (New York: Reynal & Hitchcock, 1936), pp. 250-251. Ch. 8 presents an elaborate analysis of the theses on Feuerbach.

Man makes religion, it is not religion that makes man; religion is in reality man's own consciousness and feeling which has not yet found itself or has lost itself again. . . . Man is not an abstract being outside the real world. Man is the world of men, the State, society. This State and this society produce religion, a mistaken attitude to the world, because they themselves constitute a false world. Religion is the general theory of this world, its encyclopedic compendium, its popular logic, its spiritual point of honor, its inspiration, its moral sanction, its general consoling and justifying reason. . . . It is the imaginative realization of the human essence, because that essence has no true reality. . . . It is the opium of the people.[5]

The indirect impact of Feuerbach's work has been almost as powerful as the direct. Not only did his thesis provide the Marxist movement with its fundamental attitude toward religion; it also gave to it a seemingly strong intellectual justification. And the effect of Feuerbach's ideas on many who are not communists, including many who may not even have read his works, is immeasurable. Directly or indirectly, such critics of religion as Nietzsche, Huxley, J. S. Mill, Freud, and Dewey owe basic ideas about religion to Feuerbach.

To judge rightly his thought and its implications, we must finally ask about the "Man" of whom Feuerbach writes. Religion is for him a stage in man's coming to an understanding of himself, his nature, and his tasks. But for Feuerbach (as for Comte, with whose ideas his thinking unconsciously had so much in common), religion is a stage which must be left behind. It is an illusion which binds aspiration. Man can only know himself—and become himself —by rejecting all limits to his self-assertion. He can only become great by rebelling against God. This feature, it has been pointed out, separates modern humanism from all past atheisms. "Modern humanism, then, is built upon resent-

---

[5] Karl Marx, *Contribution to the Criticism of Hegel's Philosophy,* quoted in Henri De Lubac, *The Drama of Atheist Humanism,* tr. Edith M. Riley (New York: Sheed & Ward, 1950), pp. 15-16. Marx derived the "opiate" phrase from Feuerbach.

ment and begins with a choice." [6] The term "humanism" is properly applied to Feuerbach's view, and he extols at length the virtue of love for humanity.

But is Feuerbach's view truly "humane"? The only distinction he finds in man is that between individual and species; he finds little meaning in the tension between freedom and unfreedom. For Feuerbach, as Martin Buber so rightly points out, man is not in any sense a problem for himself. [7] Feuerbach labored against the fettering of man by religious illusion. But in a situation in which this ever-present danger is perhaps not so great a threat to freedom as that of enslavement by massive political and economic systems, we may well ask whether this "humanism" has not led to an "anti-humanism." Emphasizing the species rather than the individual, and denying any species-transcending value of the human individual, Feuerbach glorifies man without reference to God. If one may judge a philosophical idea by its results, one must ask: is the "man" thus glorified really human? Can it be maintained that man is fully himself, in all his tragic glory, if he is merely a fleeting moment in time and place filled by the eternal essence of the species? Is not the next step in the history of ideas—a step beyond Feuerbach—the "unyielding despair" of existentialism and its assertion that there is no such a thing as "human nature"?

E. Graham Waring

[6] De Lubac, *op. cit.*, p. 7.
[7] Martin Buber, "What is Man?" in *Between Man and Man,* tr. Ronald Gregor Smith (Boston: Beacon Press, 1955), p. 147.

SELECTED BIBLIOGRAPHY

Ludwig Feuerbach. *Das Wesen des Christentums,* Leipzig, 1841 (Zweite vermehrte Auflage, Leipzig, 1843).

Ludwig Feuerbachs Sämtliche Werke, herausgegeben von Wilhelm Bolin und Friedrich Jodl, Stuttgart, 1903-11.

Ludwig Feuerbach. *The Essence of Christianity,* translated from the second German Edition by Marian Evans. London: Chapman, 1854. (Second edition, London: Trübner and Co., 1881. Published as Volume XV of *The English and Foreign Philosophical Library.*)

Melvin Cherno. *Ludwig Feuerbach and the Intellectual Basis of Nineteenth Century Radicalism,* Stanford University Dissertation, 1955.

Sidney Hook. *From Hegel to Marx,* New York: Humanities Press, 1950.

NOTE

This little book is an abridgment of *The Essence of Christianity*, a translation by Marian Evans, better known under her pseudonym George Eliot, of the second (1843) German edition of *Das Wesen des Christentums* by Ludwig Feuerbach.

The text presented in this volume of *Milestones of Thought* follows, in the main, George Eliot's translation. But wherever George Eliot's translation seemed inadequate, it has been revised, after careful consultation of the German original.

The sixteen chapters listed in the Table of Contents correspond as follows to the German original: Chapters 1 through 7 correspond to the same chapters in German; Chapter 8 corresponds to Chapter 12, 9 to 15, 10 to 16, 11 to 17, 12 to 19, 13 to 21, 14 to 22, 15 to 27, and 16 to 28.

The subheads interspersed within the text have been provided by the editors.

CONTENTS

THE ESSENCE OF CHRISTIANITY

Preface to the Second Edition

The clamor excited by this work has not surprised me, and hence it has not in the least moved me from my position. On the contrary, I have once more, in all calmness, subjected my work to the severest scrutiny, both historical and philosophical. I have, as far as possible, freed it from its defects of form and enriched it with new developments, new illustrations, and new historical evidence, evidence most striking and irrefutable.

Now that I have verified my analysis by historical proofs, it is to be hoped that readers who are not hopelessly blind will become convinced and admit, even if reluctantly, that my work is a faithful and correct translation of the Christian religion from the Oriental language of imagery into plain speech. My work has no pretension to be anything more than a close translation, or, to speak literally, it is meant to be merely an empirical or historical philosophical analysis of Christianity, an analysis which solves the enigma of the Christian religion.

The general propositions contained in Chapters I and II are no products of speculation; they have arisen out of the analysis of religion itself; they are only, as indeed are all the fundamental ideas of this work, generalizations drawn from the known manifestations of human nature and from man's religious consciousness in particular—they are facts converted into thought, i.e., facts expressed in general terms, and thus made the property of the understanding. The ideas of my work are only conclusions drawn from premises which are not themselves mere ideas, but objective facts either actual or historical—facts registered in volumes so big that they could not find room in my head.

I unconditionally reject pure speculation, i.e., all speculation that is self-sufficing and not based on facts—that speculation which draws its material from itself. There is a world of difference between me and those philosophers who pluck out their eyes that they may think better. When I think, I need my senses, especially sight, for I base my ideas on factual material, and that can be appropriated only through the activity of the senses. I do not generate the object from the thought, but the thought from the object; and I hold that alone to be an object which has an existence beyond one's own brain.

I am an idealist only in the realm of practical philosophy, that is, I do not mistake the limitations of the past and of the present for the limitations of Man and the future. On the contrary, I firmly believe that many things—yes, many things—which shortsighted and pusillanimous realists pass today for flights of the imagination, for unrealizable ideas or even for wild phantasies, will tomorrow, i.e., in the next century—for centuries in terms of individual life are merely days in the life of humanity—exist in full reality.

I am nothing but a natural philosopher in the domain of the mind. Not to invent, but to discover, "to unveil existence," has been my sole object; to see correctly, my sole endeavor. It is not I, but religion, that worships man, although religion, or rather theology, denies this; it is not I, an insignificant individual, but religion itself that says: God is man, man is God; it is not I, but religion that rejects and denies the God who is *not* a man, but merely a spiritual essence—for religion makes God become man, and then makes this God, who is not distinguished from man and who has a human form, human feelings, and human thoughts, the object of its worship and veneration. I have only given away the secret of the Christian religion, only extricated its true meaning from the web of contradictions and delusions called theology; naturally, therefore, I am accused of having committed a sacrilege. If, therefore, my work is negative, irreligious, atheistic, let it be remembered that atheism—at least in the sense of this work—is the secret of religion itself, that religion itself, not indeed on the surface, but fundamentally, believes in one thing only: in the truth and divinity of human nature.

To be sure, my work is negative and destructive; but, be it observed, only in relation to the *un*human, not to the human elements of religion.

The reproach that according to my book religion is an absurdity, a nullity, a pure illusion, would be well founded only if that to which I reduce religion and which I prove to be its true object and content, namely, *man* and *anthropology*, were, according to me, an absurdity, or a nullity, or a pure illusion. But I am very far from assigning a trivial or even a subordinate significance to anthropology. Such a subordinate significance is assigned to anthropology only just so long as a theology stands above it and in opposition to it; whereas I, by reducing theology to anthropology, raise anthropology to theology, just as Christianity, by lowering God into man, made Man into god.

Religion is the dream of the human mind. But even while dreaming we are not in heaven or in the realm of Nothingness. We are right here on earth, in the realm of reality, even if we see real things not as they really are and as they must necessarily be, but in the enrapturing light of wishful imagination. Hence I do nothing more to religion than to open its eyes, or, rather, to direct its inwardly turned gaze toward what is outside, so that the object as it exists in the imagination changes into what this object is in reality.

The basic ideas of my book—though not in the form in which they are expressed and had to be expressed under present circumstances—will certainly some day become the property of all mankind.

PART ONE

*The True or Anthropological Essence
of Religion*

CHAPTER I

The Essential Nature of Man Considered Generally

> *What distinguishes man from the brutes is the awareness of a distinctive human nature transcending individuality.*

Religion has its basis in the essential difference between man and the brute: the brutes have no religion.

But what constitutes this essential difference between man and the brute? The most simple and general, and also the most popular, answer to this question is "Consciousness"! But the answer is right only if one means by "consciousness" consciousness in the strict sense: for consciousness in the sense of an awareness of self as an individual cannot be denied to the brutes. Consciousness in the strictest sense is present only in a being to whom his species, his essential nature, is an object of thought.

The brute is indeed aware of himself as an individual, but he is not aware of himself as a species. Hence the brute is without that genuine consciousness which in its nature as well as in its name is akin to science. Wherever there is consciousness, there is a capacity for science. Science is the cognizance of species. In practical life we have to do with individuals, in science with species. But only a being to whom his own species, his own nature, is an object of thought can make the essential nature of other things and beings an object of thought.

What, then, *is* the nature of Man, of which man is conscious; what constitutes the "specific" distinction, the real humanity of man?

Reason, Will, and Affection!

To a complete man belong the power of thought, the power of will, and the power of the heart. The power of thought is the light of the intellect, the power of will is energy of character, the power of the heart is love. Intellect,

7

love, and will are perfections, the perfections of the human being, nay more, they are absolute and ultimate perfections of being: the very purpose of human existence. We think in order to think, we love in order to love, and we will in order to will, i.e., in order to be free. True existence is a thinking, living, willing existence, for only that which exists for its own sake, is true, perfect, and divine. But such is love, such is reason, and such is will. The unity of love, reason, and will is the divine trinity of Man above the individual man. Reason, will, and love are not powers which a man could "possess," for he would not be a man without them, he is what he is only by them; they are the constituent elements of his nature, a nature which he neither "has" nor "makes," but which *is;* they are the powers that animate, determine, and govern him; and therefore they are divine and absolute powers, to which he can oppose no resistance.

> *This distinctive nature of human subjects is reflected even in human objects and objectives.*

Man is nothing without some "objective." The great models of humanity, such men as reveal to us the essence of man, have attested the truth of this proposition by their lives. They had only one dominant passion—the realization of the aim which was the essential object of their activity.

But the object—at least the object to which a subject stands in a necessary and essential relation—is always the subject's own nature "objectified."

We know man by his object; and in it his nature becomes evident: his object is his manifested nature and his true objective self. And this is true not merely of spiritual, but also of sensuous objects. For that man sees the sun and the moon and sees them *the way* he sees them, that is a testimony to his nature. The eye which looks into the starry heavens and sees there that light, alike useless and harmless, which has nothing in common with the earth and its necessities—this eye recognizes in that light its own (dispassionate) nature. The heavens make man aware of his destination, remind him that he is destined not merely to action, but also to contemplation. The power which our objects have over us is therefore the power of our own nature.

> *Not even in our imagination can we transcend human nature; and to the "higher" beings in which we believe we can attribute nothing better than human characteristics.*

Now every being is sufficient to itself. No being can fail to approve itself, its own nature; no being is to itself something imperfect. On the contrary, each being is in itself and for itself something perfect and has its God, its "Highest Being," in itself. The limitations of a being are cognizable only by another being which exists independently of the first on a higher level.

A thing's essence—which makes this thing what it is— is its endowment: its talent, its capacities, its riches, and its beauty. What a being's essence affirms as a positive value cannot be declared worthless by its power of understanding, for otherwise this power of understanding would no longer be the power of this particular being, but that of some other being. What measures a thing's existence also measures its understanding. A limited understanding is to a limited being no limitation. On the contrary, it is perfectly happy and satisfied with this understanding and regards, lauds, and praises it as a magnificent divine power; and its limited understanding, in turn, praises the limited being whose understanding it is.

Man cannot transcend his true nature. He may indeed by means of the imagination conceive individuals of another so-called higher kind, but even then he can never get loose from his species and his nature. The specific distinctions, those final predicates of positive value which he attributes to these higher individuals, are always qualities drawn from man's own nature—qualities in which, actually, man images and projects only himself.

CHAPTER II

The Essential Nature of Religion Considered Generally

> *The religious object of adoration is nothing but the objectified nature of him who adores.*

What we have hitherto been maintaining generally of the relation between a subject and its object, applies especially to the relation between the human subject and its religious object.

In the case of sense perception, awareness of the object is quite distinguishable from consciousness of self; but consciousness of the religious object coincides with the consciousness of self.

The object of the senses exists outside of man, the religious object exists within him; and therefore he can no more be free from it than he can be free from his own self-consciousness and conscience. The religious object is the intimate, the closest object, the one most inseparable from our inner character. "God," says Augustine, for example, "is nearer, more closely related to us, and therefore more easily known by us than sensible corporeal things." The object of the senses is in itself indifferent to us, and it depends in no way on our own moral character and judgment; but the religious object has been selected and evaluated as the most excellent, the first, the supreme being. The religious object therefore necessarily presupposes a critical judgment and a discrimination between the divine and the nondivine, between what is worthy and what is not worthy of adoration.

And here may be applied, without any qualifications, the proposition: the object of a subject is nothing else than this subject's own nature objectified. Such as are a man's thoughts and moral character, such is his God; so much worth as man has, so much and no more has his God. Man's being conscious of God is man's being conscious of himself, knowledge of God is man's knowledge of himself. By their God you know men, and by knowing men you know their God; the two are identical. God is the manifested inward nature, the expressed self of man; religion is the solemn unveiling of man's hidden treasures, the revelation of his most intimate thoughts, the open confession of what he secretly loves.

But when religion—man's consciousness of God—is designated as man's consciousness of himself, this is not to be understood as affirming that the religious person is directly aware of the fact that, when he is aware of God, he is aware of himself in his nature as man. On the contrary, ignorance of this fact is fundamental to the peculiar nature of religion. To preclude this misinterpretation of my position, it is better to say: religion is man's earliest, and still indirect, form of self-knowledge. Hence, religion everywhere precedes philosophy, in the history of the race as well as in that of the individual.

Man projects his nature into the world outside of himself before he finds it in himself. In the beginning, his own nature confronts him as a being distinct from himself. Religion is the childlike condition of humanity. And this child sees his nature, Man, outside of himself. Hence the historical progress of religion consists in this: that that which during an earlier stage of religion was regarded as something objective is now recognized as something subjective, so that that which was formerly viewed and worshipped as God is now recognized as something human. The later stage of religion recognizes the earlier stage as a stage of idolatry, a stage at which man prayed to his own nature, and at which man objectified himself without recognizing the religious object for what it was: his own nature. At a later stage, religion does reach this insight. All progress in religion tends therefore to a better understanding of what we are.

The difference between what is "divine" and what is "human" is merely the difference between the generic and the individual.

It is our task to show that the antithesis of the "divine" and "human" is altogether illusory, that it is nothing else than the antithesis between human nature and human individuals, and that, consequently, both the God and the teaching of Christianity are altogether human in origin.

Religion—at least as far as Christianity is concerned— is man's attitude to himself or, more correctly, to the nature of Man as seen by the individual. However, it is an attitude toward human nature viewed as a distinct being. For the "Divine Being" is nothing else than the nature of Man, i.e., human nature purified, freed from the imperfections of the human individual, projected into the outside, and therefore viewed and revered as a different and distinct being with a nature of its own. All the attributes of the "Divine Being" are therefore attributes of man.

To recognize the human origin of the divine predicates and to uphold at the same time the existence of an indefinable Divine Being is to become a victim of modern unbelief.

As far as these attributes of the Divine Being are concerned, their human origin is, by the way, admitted without hesitation. But it is not at all admitted that their subject, God, is also of human origin. On the contrary, the negation of the subject is branded as impiety or even as atheism, though the negation of the divine predicates escapes this charge.

But a being which has no predicates or qualities cannot possibly affect me, and what has no effect upon me, does not exist for me. Where man denies God all qualities—God himself is denied. A being without qualities is one which cannot become an object to the mind, cannot be conceived of as existing. Where man deprives God of all his qualities,

God is no longer anything more to man than a negative being.

To a truly religious person, God is not merely an indefinable something; and that for the very reason that God is to him a certain and real Being. The theory that God cannot be defined and, consequently, cannot be known by man is merely the fruit of recent times, a product of modern unbelief. The allegedly "religious" hesitation to reduce God, by the attribution of definable qualities, to a finite being, is merely the irreligious desire to forget him and to banish him from the mind.

There is, however, a milder way of denying the divine predicates than the direct one just described. Some people admit that the predicates of God are finite human qualities. But they spurn the denial of these qualities and even take them under protection. It is necessary for man, they say, to have a definite conception of God; and since he is man he can form no other than human conceptions of God. As far as God is concerned, these predicates, they admit, are, to be sure, without any objective validity; but to me, if he is to exist for me, he cannot appear otherwise than he does, namely, as a human or man-like being.

But this distinction between what God is in himself and what he is for me is an unfounded and untenable distinction. I cannot possibly know whether God is something else in himself or for himself than what he is for me. What he is to me is, to me, all that he is. In such a distinction between what a thing is in itself and what it is for us, man disregards, and attempts to transcend, himself, i.e., his own nature, the absolute measure of his being; but such transcendence is illusion, for I can make the distinction between the object as it is in itself, and the object as it is for me, only where an object might actually appear to me otherwise than it does appear. I cannot make this distinction where the object can appear to me only in one way, namely in accordance with my own nature, my absolute measure.

Wherever, therefore, this idea, that the religious predicates are "merely" anthropomorphisms, has taken possession of a man, there doubt and unbelief have vanquished his faith. And it is only inconsistence, the inconsistence typical of faintheartedness and intellectual imbecility, if a man does not proceed from this position to the complete negation of the divine predicates and from there to the negation of their subject. If you doubt the objective truth of these divine predicates, you must also doubt the objective truth of the divine subject whose predicates they are. If your predicates are mere anthropomorphisms, then the subject of them is merely an anthropomorphism, too. If love, goodness, personality, etc., are human attributes, then their subject, the existing God to whom you attribute these attributes, and the very belief that there is a God, are also anthropomorphisms—i.e., presuppositions purely human in origin.

How do you know that the belief in God is not, in the last analysis, a limitation inherent in man's power of conception? Beings higher than human, as you assume them, are perhaps so blessed in themselves and so at one with themselves that they no longer feel the tension between what they are and what it is to be a higher being. To know God and not to be God, to know what blessedness would be and not to possess it, that is a conflict and a misfortune. Higher beings do not know this conflict; they have no conception of what they are not.

You believe in love as a divine attribute because you yourself love; you believe that God is a wise, benevolent being because you know nothing better in yourself than benevolence and wisdom; and you believe that God exists and that he is therefore a subject—whatever exists is a subject, no matter whether it be defined as a substance, as a person, as a being, or as something else—because you yourself exist and are yourself a subject. You know no higher human perfection than to love, to be good, and to be wise; and likewise you know no higher bliss than to exist, to be a subject; for the consciousness of bliss is for you dependent on the awareness of being a subject, of existing. God is for you an existent, a subject, for the same reason that he is for you wise, blessed, and a person. According to our way of thinking, existence is the first datum, it constitutes the subject, the presupposition to all predicates.

Nevertheless, this distinction between the subject and the predicates is merely an apparent one. The necessity of the subject is rooted in the necessity of the predicates. The predicate determines *what* the subject is, the predicate constitutes the truth of the subject. The subject is merely the personified, existing predicate. Subject and predicate are related to each other like existence and essence. The negation of the predicates entails therefore the negation of the subject.

> *And yet God is man's "truth," i.e., he is what a "true" man ought to be. Therefore we ought to strive towards godliness, for in and through God man aims at his true self.*

Because originally only the "real"—"real" in opposition to what is merely conceived, dreamed, imagined—is "true," we believe that everything we conceive to be true is also real and has an objective existence. The idea of "being," of "existence," is the original and primitive idea of "truth." Man at first bases truth on existence; only later does he learn to make existence dependent on truth.

God is the essence of man viewed as absolute truth, i.e., as the fulfillment of what is truly human. This God, however, varies with those properties which define for men their nature and because of which they view this nature as the highest form of being. The properties, therefore, which men attribute to their God constitute for them the truth and consequently the highest possible existence. And existence, the act of being, is as varied as the qualities which determine it.

When men began to discriminate between what is fitting and what is not fitting for man, they also began to discriminate between what is fitting and what is not fitting for God. The Homeric gods eat and drink, which means that eating and drinking were considered a divine pleasure. Zeus is the strongest of all gods, because physical strength, as such, was viewed as something sublime and divine. It is this sublimity or divinity of the attributes possessed, not the possession of the attribute of divinity, which is, in a non-derivative, primary sense, true Deity, truly divine being.

Therefore, that which theology and philosophy have mistaken for God, that is not God; but what they have held not to be God, i.e., his attributes, his qualities, his specific properties, and, in general the possibilities which are real in in him, these, indeed, are God.

Therefore he alone is truly an atheist to whom the predicates of Divinity—for example, love, wisdom, justice—mean nothing; not he to whom merely the subject of these predicates is nonexistent. And in no wise does the negation of the subject necessarily involve a rejection of the predicates considered in themselves. These predicates have an intrinsic reality of their own: they force their recognition upon man by their very nature; they are self-evident truths to him; they prove and attest themselves. It does not follow that goodness, justice, and wisdom are illusions just because the existence of God is an illusion, nor would they have a claim on us merely because he existed.

It is also essential to observe, and this phenomenon is an extremely remarkable one, characterizing the very core of religion, that in proportion as God becomes more ideally human, the greater becomes the apparent difference between God and man. To enrich God, man must become poor; that God may be all, man must become nothing.

Religion denies the goodness of human nature: man is wicked, corrupt, incapable of good. On the other hand, God is completely good, is the Good Being. And religion demands that this goodness, personified as God, be a human objective. But is not thereby goodness declared to be an essential characteristic and the destination of man? Either goodness is not at all for men, or, if it is, this very fact reveals to the individual the holiness and goodness of the nature of Man. That which is absolutely opposed to my nature is not even conceivable or perceptible by me. Holiness, though a contrast to my own personality, can become my objective only because it is at one with my fundamental nature.

Holiness is a reproach to my sinfulness; by means of what is holy I recognize myself as a sinner. But while I thus blame myself, I recognize what I am not, what I *ought* to be and therefore *can* be in accordance with my destination. For any "ought" without a corresponding "can" is a ludicrous chimaera. But when I acknowledge goodness as my destination, as my law, I acknowledge it, whether consciously or unconsciously, as my own real nature. I can perceive sin as sin only when I perceive it as a contradiction between me and my real self, between what I am as an individual person and what I ought to be as a human being.

Man—this is the mystery of religion—projects his nature into objectivity, and then makes himself an object of concern for this new "subject," for this projection of his nature. For God wants man to be good. God asks that man attain perfection and beatitude, for there is no beatitude without perfection. Thus man, while he apparently humiliated himself to the lowest degree, is in truth exalted to the highest; for in and through God, man aims at himself.

CHAPTER III

God as the Objectification of the Human Intellect

It must now be shown how the various attributes of God, compared to which man is imperfect, arise by objectification of diverse human powers.

Religion is the alienation of man from himself; for man sets up God as an antithesis to himself. God is not what man is, and man is not what God is. God is the infinite, man the finite being; God is perfect, man is imperfect; God is eternal, man temporal; God is holy, man sinful; God is omnipotent, man impotent. God and man constitute an antithesis: God is absolutely positive, the realization of every perfection; man is absolutely negative, comprehending in himself every imperfection.

But in religion, man objectifies his own *latent* nature. Hence it must be proved that this antithesis, this contrast between God and man with which religion begins, is in reality a conflict between the individual and his own nature.

Such a proof must necessarily be possible. For if the divine nature, which is the object of religion, were really different from the nature of man, conflict and disunion would not be possible. If God were actually a being different from myself, why should his perfection trouble me? Disunion and conflict exist only between beings who are at variance, but who ought to be at-one, who can be at-one, and who consequently, in nature and in truth, are one.

On this general ground alone it can be assumed that that "Being" with which man feels himself in discord must necessarily be his own immanent and inborn nature. But it must be a part of our nature which is different from that other part or power which can give us the feeling of reconciliation, of being at-one with God, or, which is the same thing, of being at-one with ourselves.

> *God as a mind "beyond" human reason is an objectification of human intelligence stripped of all accidental imperfections.*

God as the antithesis of man, God seen as a nonhuman, i.e., as a not individually human being, is the projected objective nature of intelligence. The divine being in its unadulterated perfection is the intellect conscious of itself and of its perfection.

The intellect in us is neutral, dispassionate, unbribable and unblinded, it is that unadulterated light of intelligence which cannot be led astray by passion. Only by means of the intellect can man judge and act contrary to his dearest personal human feelings whenever this intellect-god, i.e., law, necessity, and justice, commands it. A father who in his capacity as judge condemns his own son to death because he recognizes the son's guilt, can do this only as a rational, not as an emotional being.

For the intellect is the power keyed to what is nonindividual. While our heart pleads for particular interests, for individuals, our intellect defends what is of and in the common interest. The intellect is the superhuman, i.e., the super-personal and impersonal power in man. It is only by means of his intellect that the individual can free himself from himself, from his individual characteristics, that he can lift himself to concepts and patterns of general validity, that he can distinguish a thing from the impact it has on our emotions and view this thing as it is in itself, apart from all relation to human beings. Philosophy, mathematics, astronomy, physics, in short, science in general, is the factual proof of this assertion, for science is the product of this truly divine activity. Neither does the intellect tolerate religious anthropomorphism. It denies that God is human. Naturally! For this nonhuman, relentless, passionless God is in reality merely the projected nature of the intellect itself.

God as God, i.e., God as a nonfinite, nonhuman, non-material, and nonphenomenal being, is exclusively an object of thought. He is "in"corporeal, form"less," "in"comprehensible and "non"picturable; he can be known and become an object to me only by my stating what he is not (*via negationis*).

Why?

Because he is nothing but the objectified nature of our power of thought. Man cannot possibly believe in, imagine, suspect, or conceive of any other kind of intellect or intelligence than that which enlightens him and is active in him. He can only separate this intelligence from the limitations of his own individuality. In contrast to the "finite" mind, the "in"finite mind is therefore nothing but intelligence separated in thought from the limitations of individuality and corporeality.

God as God, that is, God as a being which one can only think and which is an object only to the intellect, is therefore nothing else than this intellect itself, depicting itself in perfection as its own object. God is Reason declaring and affirming itself as the "Highest Being."

According to our phantasies and imagination, God reveals what he is through the nature of human reason; but according to rational analysis human reason reveals itself through God, for what reason is and what it can do is not made manifest until objectified in God. Not until our thought is God, do we attain an adequate conception of the true nature of Reason in spite of the fact that, through imagination, we erroneously attribute to this only-in-thought-existing-being again individual existence. Reason is the criterion for what can be and what cannot be real. Whatever contradicts reason, whatever is self-contradictory, is incompatible with God. Reason can only believe in a God who is in accordance with its own nature, in a God who is not beneath its own dignity, who, on the contrary, is a realization of its own nature; i.e., reason believes only in itself, in the absolute affirmation of its essence. What, therefore, do you affirm, what do you objectify in God? Your own reason! God is your highest idea, the highest conception of your intellect, the highest conception you can possibly have. What I recognize as belonging to the essence of reason I posit in God as existing.

The measure of your God is determined by your own reason. If you conceive God as limited, then your reason is limited. When you deny that God is corporeal, you merely prove and practice by this denial the freedom of your reason from the limitations of corporeality. The "boundless Being" merely objectifies your own unbounded reason.

CHAPTER IV

God as a Moral Being or Law

God as the impassionate mind is not the answer to religious yearning.

God as God—i.e., God as the infinite, nonindividual, nonanthropomorphic nature of the intellect—has no more significance for religion than a fundamental general principle has for a special science: he is merely the ultimate point of support; he is for religion, so to speak, what the point is for mathematics.

The awareness of human limitation and worthlessness which is inseparable from the belief in this being is by no means pious, religious consciousness. On the contrary, this awareness characterizes the skeptic, the materialist, and the pantheist: for faith and trust in God—at least in the God of religion—are lost wherever, as in skepticism, pantheism, and materialism, faith in man is lost. To the extent, therefore, that religion cannot possibly take the complete worthlessness of man seriously, it cannot take that abstract being seriously on which the consciousness of this worthlessness depends. Religion takes only those attributes of God seriously which make Man an object of man. To reject Man is to repudiate religion.

To be sure, it is in the interest of religion that the being which is its object should be distinct from the believer; but it is also, indeed more, in its interest that this other being should, at the same time, be human. That God should be a distinct being concerns his existence only, but that he should be human concerns his inner essence. If he were really an "other" being, i.e., a being of a different nature, how could his existence or nonexistence be of any concern to man?

In religion man seeks peace and contentment; religion

is his highest good. But how could he find consolation and peace in God, if God were essentially an "other," a non-human being? How can I share the peace of God, if I do not share his nature? If his nature is different from mine, his peace also is essentially different—and no peace for me. Every Being experiences peace only in its own nature. Thus, if we feel peace in God, we feel it only because God alone is our true nature, because only here we are with ourselves, because everything else in which we hitherto sought peace and which we hitherto mistook for our nature was actually alien to us. Hence, if man is to, and wants to, find peace in God, he must find in God—himself!

A God, therefore, who objectifies merely the nature of the intellect does not satisfy religion and is not the God of religion. For the intellect is interested not merely in man, but also in things not human, in Nature. The intellectual man even forgets himself in the contemplation of Nature. But it is a characteristic mark of religion, and of the Christian religion especially, that it is rooted exclusively in man's love for himself and in man's affirmation of the human, the individual human being. Hence not the objectified nature of the intellect but something else must become the God of religion before man can find peace in religion, and this something will necessarily be the very kernel of religion.

> *But God is not only an objectification of man's intellect, he also is a personification of man's moral conscience.*

Of all the attributes which reason and intellect assign to God, moral perfection is the one most important for religion, and especially for the Christian religion. But God as a morally perfect being is nothing else than the realized idea and the fulfilled law of morality. God is the moral nature of man posited as the absolute being. He is man's own nature, for this moral God requires man to be as he himself is: "Be ye holy for I am holy." He is man's own conscience, for how could man otherwise tremble before the

Divine Being, accuse himself before him, and make him the judge of his inmost thoughts and feelings?

But I cannot form the ideal of moral perfection without at the same time becoming aware of the fact that this perfection constitutes a law for me.

Moral perfection resides, at least for the moral consciousness, not in one's nature, but in one's will. Moral perfection is a perfection of will, it is the perfect will. I cannot conceive this perfect will, this will which is at-one with the Law and which is itself the Law, without at the same time regarding such a will as an objective for my will, i.e., as an obligation for myself. In short, the conception of the morally perfect being is no merely theoretical, no inert ideal. It is a practical ideal calling me to action, to imitation, throwing me into strife and into conflict with myself. For while this ideal proclaims to me what I ought to be, it also tells me to my face and without any flattery what I am not. And religion renders this conflict all the more painful, all the more terrible, because it sets man's own nature before him as a distinct being, as a personal being, moreover, who hates and curses sinners and excludes them from his grace, the source of all salvation and happiness.

Now, by what means does man deliver himself from this conflict between his own self and this perfect being? By what means can man free himself from the painful consciousness of sin, and from the distressing sense of his own worthlessness? How does he blunt the fatal sting of sin? Only by realizing that the heart, that love is the greatest, the absolute power and the highest, the absolute truth; only by regarding the Divine Being not merely as a law, as a moral being, or as an intellect, but rather as a loving, tender human individual.

> *It is the attribution of love, and of flesh and blood, to God which establishes a real bond between man and man's God. For this incarnate God is himself human and no longer inhuman.*

The intellect judges only according to the stringency of the law; the heart makes concessions, is considerate, lenient, relenting, human. No man is acceptable to the law, which demands no less than moral perfection of us. However, for that very reason, neither is the law acceptable to man and his heart. The law condemns; the heart has compassion even on the sinner. The law approves only what is nonindividual in me; love approves me in my individual reality. Love makes me aware that I am human; the law only makes me aware that I am a sinner and that I am worthless. The law subjects man to itself; love makes him free.

Love makes man divine, and it makes God human.

A merely moral judge, who does not infuse human blood into his judgment, judges the sinner relentlessly and without forgiveness. Therefore, by regarding God as a sin-pardoning being, God is posited, not indeed as an immoral, but as a not merely moral, as a more than moral, in a word, as a human, being. The annulling of sin is the annulment of abstract moral righteousness, the recognition of love, mercy, and sensuous life.

Not abstract beings—no! only sensuous, living beings are merciful. Mercy is the justice of sensuous life. Hence it is not God as the abstract God of the intellect, but God as man, God as the God made flesh, God as a physical being, who finds in himself forgiveness for the sins of men. This God-man, it is true, does not sin, but he knows and takes upon himself the sufferings, the wants, and the agony of sensuous beings. The blood of Christ cleanses us from our sins in the eyes of God; for it is only his human blood that makes God merciful and allays his anger.

CHAPTER V

The Mystery of the Incarnation

> *The doctrine of Incarnation, though misunderstood by religion, raises purified humanity to the level of loveworthy divinity.*

As long as one defines the incarnation merely as "God-becoming-man," the incarnation is, I admit, a surprising, unexplainable, and miraculous event. We must not forget, however, that the "God-who-became-man" is merely the appearance of the "Man-who-became-God"; for the descent of God to man was necessarily preceded by the exaltation of man to God. Man was already in God, was already God himself, before God became man, i.e., revealed himself as man.

The statement "God is or becomes man" is mysterious, incomprehensible, and, as a matter of fact, contradictory, only because we confuse the demands of the intellect and its conception of a nonindividual, perfect, nonphysical being with the demands of the heart and its conception of a God as an object for religion.

Church doctrine takes cognizance of this difficulty by stating that it was not the first, but the second person of the trinity, who became man. Actually this second person, as we shall show, is the first, the whole, and the only truly divine person for the pious heart.

> *Though theology does not realize it, man, by positing Christ as the God incarnate, has proclaimed that man's selfless love for humanity constitutes salvation.*

The essential idea of the Incarnation, though enveloped in the darkness of religious consciousness, is love. Love determined God to renounce his divinity. It was not because of his Godhead, as such, according to which he is the *subject* in the proposition "God is love," but because of his love, because of the *predicate*, that he renounced his deity or Godhead. Thus love is a higher power and truth than deity. Love conquers God. It was love to which God sacrificed his divine majesty. And what sort of love was that? Love of another kind than ours? A love different from that to which we sacrifice life and fortune? Was it love of himself, of himself as God? No! It was love for man.

But is not love for man human love? Can I really love man without loving him in a human way, i.e., without loving him the way he himself loves whenever he truly loves? Would not love be otherwise a devilish love? After all, the devil loves man, too. But not for the sake of man, but for his own, the devil's sake; out of egotism, in other words, and in order to aggrandize himself and to enlarge his power. But God, in his love for man, loves man for man's sake, in order to make man good, happy, and even blessed. Does he therefore not love man the way a true man loves man? Does "love" have a plural form? Is it not everywhere the same?

Though there is also a self-interested love among men, still, truly human love, which alone is worthy of the name "love," is that which impels the sacrifice of self to another.

Who then is our Savior and Redeemer? God or love? Love! And as God has renounced himself out of love, so we, out of love, should renounce God; for if we do not sacrifice God to love, we sacrifice love to God, and, in spite of his predicate of love, we have the God—the evil being—of religious fanaticism.

The incarnation of love on earth passes away, but love remains. Its appearance was limited by time and place, accessible to few. However, the essence manifested is eternal and universal. We should still believe in this manifestation, not for the sake of the manifestation but for the sake of the thing manifested, for all that remained for us is the vision of love.

If the object of God's love is man, is not then man, in God, an object to himself? If God is Love, and if the essential object of this love is man, is not then the inner essence of the Divine Being human nature? Is not then the love of God for man, the kernel and center of religion, the love of man for himself, objectified and recognized as the highest objective Truth, as the highest realization of human nature? Is not then the proposition "God loves man" an Orientalism which means in plain speech: there is nothing higher than man's love for man?

CHAPTER VI

The Mystery of the Suffering God

*Not even suffering and fear of suffering, insepa-
rable from human nature, are alien to the incarnate
God created by religious yearning.*

An essential characteristic of the incarnate, or, what is
the same thing, of the human, God, namely, of Christ, is the
Passion.

Love attests itself by suffering.

All the thoughts and feelings which we have when we
think of Christ center on the idea of the Passion. God as God
is the sum of all human perfection; God as Christ is the sum
of all human misery. The heathen philosophers glorified activity, especially the spontaneous activity of intelligence, as
something divine; the Christians consecrated suffering and
posited it even in God.

Now according to the principles which we have already
developed, we can take it for granted that what in religion
is taken to be the predicate is actually the subject, and that
what in religion is taken to be the subject is actually the
predicate. It is by inverting the oracles of religion that we
arrive at the truth. "God suffers"—suffering is the predicate!
But he suffers for men, for others, not for himself. What
does that mean in plain speech? Nothing else than "to
suffer for others is divine." He who suffers for others and
lays down his life for them acts divinely and is therefore to
men—God!

The Passion of Christ, however, represents not only the
moral, voluntary act of suffering out of a love strong enough
to enable him to sacrifice himself for the good of others;
Christ's passion represents also suffering as such, i.e., suffering as a manifestation of the capacity to suffer.

29

The Christian religion is so far from being superhuman that it even sanctions human weakness. While Socrates empties the cup of poison with unshaken soul, Christ exclaims, "If it be possible, let this cup pass from me." Christ is in this respect the self-confession of the human capacity for feeling. In opposition to the heathens, and in particular to stoicism with its rigorous energy of will and self-sustainedness, the Christians have included the consciousness of their own sensitiveness and susceptibility in their conception of God. If only weakness be no sinful weakness, they find it not denied to God and not condemned in God.

Religion is human nature reflected and mirrored in itself. Whatever exists, likes itself, rejoices in what it is, and loves itself. And it loves itself justly. If you blame a being for this love, you blame it for the fact that it exists. Wherever, therefore, feeling is not looked down upon and suppressed, as was the case among the stoics, wherever feeling is permitted to exist, there also religious significance and importance are conceded to feeling, there feeling has already been exalted to that stage on which it can project, and reflect itself in, its own image, so that it can see in God, as in a mirror, itself. *God is the mirrored image of man.*

CHAPTER VII

The Mystery of the Trinity

> *Just as man projects himself into the "outside" and thereby posits God, so God, according to theology, projects himself and thereby generates the Son. Thus the one God becomes two Persons.*

If a God without feeling and without a capability of suffering will not suffice to man because man is a feeling and suffering being, neither will a God with feeling only, a God without intelligence and moral will. Only a divine Being who comprises in himself the whole man can satisfy the whole man.

Man's consciousness of himself in his totality is man's consciousness of the Trinity.

The concept of the Trinity makes a unified "One" out of the various qualities and powers which we have analyzed separately in the preceding chapters, and it thereby reduces the nonindividual nature of the intellect—and thereby God as God—to a particular person with a particular faculty.

God thinks and loves. But he thinks and loves himself; and what he thinks and what he loves confronts him as a real being which is itself God, and God himself. The objectification of the knowledge that God has of himself is the first thing to be noted in the Trinity.

Thus a second being, a being of identically the same nature as God, but distinct from God by being not the same person, is posited into the still solitude of the Deity: God the Son, distinct from God the Father.

> *By projecting his own yearning for fellowship into God, man posits a third Person, the Spirit of love,*

> *into the Deity, and thereby establishes a link be-*
> *tween the first and the second Person.*

God the Father is I, God the Son Thou. The I is the understanding intellect, the Thou is love. But a love rooted in understanding or an understanding rooted in love is what we mean by spirituality, and spirituality constitutes the totality of man as man.

Only a life in fellowship is truly life, satisfying in itself, and divine.

Religion expresses this truth, as it expresses every other truth, only indirectly and in an upside-down manner. For it again changes the real subject into a mere predicate by saying: God is a life in fellowship, God is the living realization of love. Actually the third person of the Trinity [the Spirit of Love] merely expresses the love of the first two Persons toward each other, a love illogically posited as another distinct personal being.

The Christians, and I mean of course the ancient Christians who would hardly recognize the vain, heathen, and secularized Christians of our modern age as brethren in Christ, rejected real family life and the intimate bond of natural love as godless, as worthless, and as unfit for heaven. In compensation, they had in God a Father and a Son who embraced each other with heartfelt love, with that intensive love which is possible only between persons of a like nature. Here, in their Deity, they could view the satisfaction of those deep-seated human needs which they rejected in real life; and for that reason the mystery of the Trinity filled them with excessive admiration, enthusiasm, and rapture.

A son—I mean a natural, human son—is, so to speak an intermediate being between the masculine nature of the father and the feminine nature of the mother; he is, as it were, still half man, half woman, inasmuch as he has not the full, rigorous awareness of independence which characterizes the man, and feels himself drawn rather to the mother than to the father. The love of the son to the mother is the first love of the masculine being to the feminine.

Necessarily, therefore, the idea of the Mother of God is associated with the idea of the Son of God. The same human heart that needed the one needed the other also.

Where faith in the Mother of God declines, there also declines faith in the Son of God and in God the Father. The Father is a truth only where the Mother is a truth.

Protestantism has set aside the Mother of God. But the neglected woman has had her revenge: the weapons that Protestantism used against the Mother of God have turned against itself, against the Son and the whole Trinity.

The triune God is the God of Catholicism. He has a profound, heartfelt, truly religious significance, and is, therefore, a religious need only when real life is emptied of its meaning. The more empty life becomes, the richer and fuller becomes God. The impoverishing of the real world and the enriching of the Deity is one and the same act. Only an impoverished humanity has a rich God.

The triune God springs out of a feeling of want. What man misses—whether this be an articulate and therefore conscious, or an unconscious, need—that is his God. The disconsolate feeling of emptiness and loneliness demands a God in whom there is fellowship, a union of beings fervently in love with each other.

CHAPTER VIII

The Significance of the Dogma of Creation in the Hebrew Religion

The dogma of creation, taken over by Christianity from the Hebrews, is an expression of egotism and possible only when man feels himself no longer a part of Nature.

The doctrine of creation had its origin in Judaism. Its underlying principle is egotism.

The doctrine of creation in the theological meaning of the term can arise only where man, with a pragmatic attitude, looks upon Nature merely as a means for the satisfaction of his needs, subjects it to his own will, and thereby degrades Nature even in his thought to a mere "fabrication," to the mere "product" of a will.

As a matter of fact, the question, "Where did the universe come from?" presupposes astonishment over the fact that it exists. It also presupposes the question, "Why does it exist?"

But this astonishment and this question can arise only where man has separated himself from Nature and where he has degraded Nature to a mere object of will. The author of the *Book of Wisdom* remarks quite correctly that the heathens, because they were so preoccupied with admiring the beauty of the world, never rose to the concept of a Creator. For to him for whom Nature is something beautiful, Nature is an end in itself and needs no reason, no purpose, for its existence. The question, "Why does it exist?" will never occur to such a person. To be sure, this Nature, as it affects his senses, has indeed an origin, has come into being by "generation," but it was not, at least not in the strict

34

religious sense of the term, "created"; it was not "made," it is no arbitrary "product." Neither does coming-into-being-by-generation express or imply for such a person something evil, something unclean, and something ungodly. He even imagines his gods as having come into being. Generative power is to him the basic primeval force. And this natural force, real, present everywhere, and active before his very eyes, is assumed by him to be the very foundation and cause of Nature. And men think this way, wherever they take an aesthetic or disinterested scientific attitude towards the world.

Wherever, on the other hand, man takes a narrowly practical point of view, actually looks at the world from this position, and even substitutes the practical for the scientific point of view, he is no longer in union with Nature, makes Nature the abject vassal of his selfish interest, of his practical egotism.

The theoretical expression of this practical, egotistical point of view, from which Nature has no value in and for itself, is the formula: the world was made, it was created, it is the product of an order. God spoke, "Let the world be," and the world began to be; God ordered, "Let the world begin to exist," and it promptly reported for existence.

The Greeks cultivated the humanities, the fine arts, and philosophy The Hebrews never outgrew theology, the study of how to keep oneself well fed: "At even ye shall eat flesh, and in the morning ye shall be filled with bread; and ye shall know that I am the Lord your God." (Exodus 16,12)

The history of dogma differs in no way from the history of states. An institution that was once good, claims to be good for all times. Whatever has come into existence, claims the right to exist forever; and finally the dreamers and the interpreters arrive and start talking about the profound sense of a custom or institution, because they no longer know the true one. Theological speculation is no different:

analyzing dogmas isolated from the context in which alone they have a meaning, it fails to trace these dogmas by critical methods to their true origin.

But it is only in the origin of the thing that one can discern its true nature. First, man, without knowing it and without wanting to, created God in his image; and thereafter did this God knowingly and willingly create man in his image. This fact is corroborated above all by the development of Hebrew religion. The "supernatural" egotism of the Hebrews did not spring from the Creator. It was the other way around. The Hebrews justified their egotism before the throne of reason by the doctrine of creation. We need only drop the limitations imposed by nationalism, and we get Christianity.

CHAPTER IX

The Mystery of Christ's Resurrection

The dogma that Christ arose from the dead is a result of wishful thinking: Men want to be certain of a continued existence after death.

All human beings, at least as long as they are healthy, desire not to die. Originally, this wish is identical with the instinct of self-preservation. Everything that lives seeks to maintain itself, wants to live, and consequently does not want to die. Later on, when reflection and feeling are developed under the pressure of life in general, and of social and political life in particular, this at first purely negative wish not to die becomes positive and changes into the desire for a better life after death.

This wish implies the further wish for the certainty of its fulfillment. Reason cannot provide this certainty. It has, therefore, been said that all proofs of immortality lack cogency. It has even been said that reason, by itself, is not capable of apprehending, still less of proving, the immortality of the individual. And this is correct; for reason furnishes only proofs dealing with what is nonindividual; reason cannot give me the certainty of my own personal, individual immortality—and it is precisely this certainty which the individual demands.

Such certainty requires a direct personal assurance, a practical demonstration. This can be given to me only when a dead person, whose death has previously been certified, rises again from the grave. This person, furthermore, cannot be just anybody; he must, on the contrary, be someone who is the type, the precursor, and the representative of all others, so that his resurrection also will be a prefiguration, and therefore a guarantee, of their resurrection. The resurrection of Christ is therefore the satisfaction of man's desire for the immediate certainty of his personal existence after death. Christ's resurrection proves personal immortality to be an unquestionable physical fact.

Among the heathen philosophers immortality was a question in which personal interest was merely a collateral point. They concerned themselves chiefly with the nature of the soul, the nature of the mind, and the nature of the vital principle. The idea of the continued existence of the vital principle by no means involves the idea, not to mention the certainty, of personal immortality. Hence the vagueness, the discrepancy, and the dubiousness with which the ancients express themselves on this subject.

The Christians, on the other hand, who were certain that their personal, emotional desires would be fulfilled, that their emotions were of divine nature, and that their personal feelings were true and unassailable, converted the merely theoretical hypothesis of the ancients into an immediate fact, converted a theoretical and in itself open question into a binding dogma, the denial of which was equivalent to the high treason of atheism.

CHAPTER X

The Mystery of the Christian Redeemer

The Christian theory of justification by faith is rooted in a cowardly renunciation of moral effort.

The fundamental dogmas of Christianity are realized wishes of the human heart: the essence of Christianity is the essence of what the human heart desires.

It is pleasanter and less exerting to be passive than to act; pleasanter to be redeemed and to be made free by another than to free oneself; pleasanter to make one's salvation dependent on a person than dependent on the strength of one's own endeavor; pleasanter to set before oneself an object of love than an object of effort; pleasanter to know oneself beloved by God than merely to love oneself with that simple, natural self-love which is innate in all things. And to see one's image reflected in the love-beaming eyes of another person is more pleasant than to look into the concave mirror of one's own self or into the cold depth of the ocean of Nature.

The highest demand of the heart and its wishful thinking is that there should be an immediate unity of wish and reality, of will and deed.

This demand is fulfilled by the Redeemer.

Just as physical miracles, in contrast to natural activity, realize immediately the physical wants and wishes of men, so the Redeemer, the Atoner, the God-man, in contrast to the moral efforts of men who act in accordance with Nature or reason, satisfies immediately our deep-seated moral desires and needs by dispensing men from any intermediate activity to be performed by themselves.

What you desire has already been effected.

You desire to earn, to deserve happiness? Morality is

the condition of happiness, the means by which happiness may be attained! But you cannot possibly fulfill this condition; and, as a matter of fact, you need not fulfill it yourself. What you seek has already been done. You need only be passive, you need only believe, you need only enjoy. You desire to make God inclined toward you, to appease his anger, and to be at peace with your conscience? But this peace exists already, this peace is the Mediator, the God-man! He is your appeased conscience, he is the fulfillment of the Law and thereby the fulfillment of your own wishing and striving.

For this very reason it is now no longer the law but the fulfiller of the law who is the model, the rule, and the law of your life. For he who fulfills the law annuls the law; and he who fulfills it completely can say to the law: What you want me to do, I want to do anyhow, and what you command me to do I affirm by my actions; my life is the true, the living law.

The fulfiller of the law therefore necessarily steps into the place of the law. Moreover, he becomes a new law, a law whose yoke is light and easy. For the law, which merely demands obedience, is now replaced by him who presents himself to us as an example and as an object of our love, of our admiration and imitation; and thus he frees us from sin. For the law itself does not give me the strength to fulfill it. On the contrary! It is barbaric and commands, without paying the slightest attention to the question whether I can, and how I ought to, fulfill the law. The law leaves me to myself, without counsel or aid. But he whose example lights up my path takes me by the hand and bestows upon me his strength. The law is powerless against sin, but the example effects miracles. The law calls only on my intellect and sets itself directly in opposition to my instincts. The example, on the other hand, makes use of a powerful natural instinct: the instinct for imitation. In short, the example has magical, i.e., sense-affecting powers.

It is necessary, however, to point out that the power of

the virtuous example is not so much the power of virtue as the power of example in general. To be sure, the virtuous example may elicit virtuous acts, but only acts performed without virtue functioning as the inner motivating power.

The miraculous redeemer is merely a realization of the desire to be free from the laws of morality and to be exempt from those conditions under which alone virtue can be attained in the natural course of things. Christ is the realization of the desire to be freed from moral evils instantaneously, immediately, and by a stroke of magic, that is in an absolutely subjective, easy way.

"God's word," says Luther, "accomplishes all things without delay. The forgiveness of sins and the eternal life it brings to you cost you nothing more than this: You must hear the word and believe it when you have heard it. If you do believe it, you have it without effort, without cost, without delay, and without hardship."

Christ, therefore, is the blessed certainty that God is, and that he is what our wishful heart desires and needs him to be.

CHAPTER XI

The Distinction between Christianity and Heathenism

> *Since the Christian God is a generic concept made into an individual person, Christianity loses the distinction between the individual and the species and over-evaluates the individual.*

The idea of deity coincides with the idea of humanity. All divine attributes, all the attributes which make God God, are attributes of the species—attributes which in the individual are limited, but the limits of which are abolished in the essence of the species. My knowledge, my will, is limited; but my limit is not the limit of another human being, to say nothing of mankind; what is difficult to me is easy to another; what is impossible, inconceivable, to one age, is to the coming age conceivable and possible. My life is bound to a limited time; not so the life of humanity. The history of mankind consists of nothing else than a continuous and progressive conquest of limits which, at a given time, are taken to be the limits of humanity, and therefore absolute and insurmountable. But the future always unveils the fact that the alleged limits of the species were only limits of individuals. It is only the individual which is limited; the species is unlimited.

But the awareness of limitation is painful, and hence the individual frees himself from it by contemplating the Perfect Being. In this contemplation he possesses what otherwise is wanting in him. With the Christians, God is nothing else than the immediate unity of species and individuality, of generic and individual existence.

God is the "individualized" idea of the species, i.e., he is the idea or the essence of the species, and yet, though species, though a nonindividual generic being, he is at the same time an individual, personal being. *Ipse suum esse est:* "Essence and existence coincide in God,"—which simply means: he is a generic being, a generic concept which, at the same time, has actual existence not just indirectly in individuals, but directly as an individual. From the point of view of religion, the highest thought is this: God does not love, he is love; he does not live, he is life; he is not just, but justice itself; and he is not a person, but personality itself, i.e., the species, the idea of a person existing as a concrete individual.

But because of this immediate unity of the generic and the individual, because of this concentration of all generic perfections in one personal being, God is a deeply moving object, enrapturing to the imagination; whereas the idea of humanity or human-ness has little power over our feelings because human-ness is to our mind only an abstraction. The reality which presents itself to us in distinction from this abstraction is the multitude of separate, limited individuals.

Nevertheless, God is merely man's vision of his own, i.e., man's nature. Thus the Christians are distinguished from the heathens by the fact that they immediately identify the individual with the species, that for them the individual has the significance of the species, and that the individual by himself is held to be the perfect representative of the species—that they deify the human individual.

The heathens considered the individual man only in connection with other men, i.e., in connection with society. They rigorously distinguished the individual from the species, viewed the individual as a part of the whole of humanity and subordinated that part to the whole. Though they thought highly of the race, highly of the excellency of what it means to be a human being, highly of the intelligence, they nevertheless thought slightly of the individual. Christianity, on the other hand, cared nothing for the species, and had only the individual in its eye and mind. The ancients sacrificed the individual to the species; the Christians sacrificed the species to the individual.

The exaggeration of the importance of the individual leads to an exaggeration of the importance of sin.

The total absence of the idea of the species in Christianity is especially observable in its characteristic doctrine of the universal sinfulness of men.

What is entirely lacking in this doctrine is the realization and the awareness of the fact that the *thou* belongs to the perfection of the *I*, that only all men together constitute humanity, and that only all men taken together are what Man should and can be.

I grant that all men are sinners. But they are not all sinners in the same way. On the contrary, there exists a great and essential difference between them. One man is inclined to falsehood, another is not: he would rather give up his life than break his word or tell a lie. The third has a propensity to intoxication, the fourth to licentiousness; while the fifth, whether by the favor of Nature or from the energy of his character, exhibits none of these vices. Thus, in the moral as well as in the physical and intellectual realm, men compensate for each other, so that, taken as a whole, they are as they should be: representing Man in his perfection.

But if human beings, who are imperfect individuals, constitute through love and friendship a relatively perfect whole, how much more do the sins and failings of individuals vanish in the species itself, which has its adequate existence only in the sum total of all mankind. Hence the lamentation over sin is found only when the human individual regards himself in his individuality as a perfect, complete being, as a being which does not need others for the realization of the species, for the realization of Man in his perfection. It is found only where the individual, not admitting that he is merely a part of mankind, identifies himself with the species.

There is a qualitative, critical difference between men.

But Christianity extinguishes this qualitative distinction; it sets the same stamp on all men alike, and regards them as one and the same individual because it knows no distinction between the species and the individual: it has one and the same means of salvation for all men, it sees one and the same original sin in all.

Because Christianity, from exaggerated subjectivity, knows nothing of the species, in which alone lie the redemption, the justification, the atonement, and the annulment for the sins and deficiencies of the individual, it needs a supernatural and peculiar, nay, a personal, individual aid in order to overcome sin. If I alone am the species, if no qualitatively different men exist, if my sins are not neutralized by the opposite qualities of other men, then assuredly my sin is a blot of shame which cries up to heaven, a revolting horror which can be exterminated only by extraordinary, superhuman, miraculous means. Happily, however, there *is* a natural atonement: my fellowman is *per se* the mediator between me and the sacred idea of the species. *Homo homini Deus est:* Man is man's Redeemer. My sin is thrust into nothingness by the fact that it is only mine and not that of my fellow men.

CHAPTER XII

The Christian Heaven and Personal Immortality

> *The desire to claim for the individual what belongs only to the species finds its strongest expression in the doctrine of immortality, according to which the blessed will be what God is.*

The Christians have abolished the difference and the distinction between the species and the individual, and directly claim for their own individual selves what belongs only to the totality of the species. But, as we have seen, the immediate unity of species and individuality is Christianity's highest principle, its deity. In Christianity, the individual has the significance of the Absolute Being; and the necessary consequence of this principle is personal immortality.

Our own future nature, which is not yet ours while we are in this world and in this body, and which is present to us only as our ideal objective, that is—God. God is the idea of the species which will be individualized and realized, realized in us, only in heaven. He is the pure, free, heavenly essence which will gain existence in heaven in a multitude of pure beings. He is the bliss which will unfold itself there in blissful individuals. This is clearly expressed in the belief that beatitude consists in unity with God. Here on earth, we are different and separated from God, there the partition falls; here we are men, there we will be gods; while we are here, Godhead is a monopoly, there it will be a common possession.

The identity of the divine personality and the heavenly human personality is apparent even in the popular proofs of immortality: "If there is no other and better life, God is not just and good." The justice and goodness of God are thus made dependent on the continued existence of individuals. But God without justice and goodness is not God; the existence of God and his God-ness is therefore made dependent on the existence of individuals. If I am not immortal, I do not believe in God; he who denies immortality denies the existence of God. The interest I have in God's existence is identical with the interest I have in my own eternal existence. God represents the existence which corresponds to my feelings and my desires. The world of Nature is an existence contrary to my feelings and desires. Here on earth, things are not what they ought to be, and therefore this world will pass away; but God, Deity, is existence as it ought to be.

The doctrine of immortality is the final doctrine of religion. It is the testament in which religion declares its last will. In this doctrine, therefore, it expresses undisguisedly what it otherwise suppresses. While the religious soul concerns itself elsewhere with the existence of another being, it concerns itself here openly only with its own existence. While elsewhere in religion man makes his existence dependent on the existence of God, he makes here the reality of God dependent on his own reality.

> *At the same time the belief in a better life hereafter is an escape mechanism, which prevents men from going after a better life in a straight line. Religion is as bad as opium.*

The belief in heaven and, in general, the belief in a future life rests on a judgment. The belief expresses both blame and praise. That which man thinks beautiful, good, and agreeable, is for him what alone ought to be; that which he thinks bad, odious, and disagreeable, is that which ought not to be and which therefore, since it exists nevertheless, is worthless and condemned to destruction. Where life is not judged to disagree with our feelings, our conceptions, and our ideas, and where these feelings, conceptions, and ideas are not taken to be absolutely true and justified, the belief in another and a heavenly life does not arise. For this other life is nothing else than a life in accordance with those desires and ideas with which the present life conflicts. The hereafter has no other function than that of abolishing this conflict and of realizing a state which corresponds to our desires and in which we are at-one with ourselves.

With "savage" tribes, belief in a future world and in a life after death is essentially nothing more than unbroken faith in this life. For them, their actual life, even with its local limitations, has absolute value, and they believe actually that this life will go on and never come to an end. Only when the belief in immortality becomes a critical belief, when a distinction is made between what is to be left behind here, and what is to continue to exist there, between what is to perish here and what is to abide there, only then belief in life after death becomes belief in a different kind of life. Nevertheless this criticism and this distinction make themselves felt already in this life. Thus Christians make a distinction between a life which is natural, sensual, and worldly, and a life which is Christian, spiritual, and holy. The "other" life in heaven is really not "other" at all. It is only the spiritual life which is already here distinguished from the merely natural life, only the spiritual life here is still tainted with the natural life. What the Christian excludes from himself here, the sexual life for example, that is also excluded from the "other" life. The only difference is that he is there actually free from the things which he desires to be free from while on earth, and which he seeks to rid himself of by will, devotion, and mortification.

Belief in a life hereafter is therefore only faith in what would truly be life here and now. The essential elements of this life are also the essential elements of the other life. Belief in a future life is therefore not belief in some other, as yet unknown, life, but belief in the truth and the perpetuity of that life which, while still here on earth, is regarded as the authentic life.

Just as God is nothing else than the nature of man purified of everything which appears to the individual as a limitation or an evil, so the future life is nothing else than life here and now freed from everything that appears a limitation or an evil. The more definitely and profoundly the individual is conscious of the limitation as a limitation, of the evil as an evil, the more definite and profound is his conviction of the future life where these limitations will disappear. The only difference between the course of religion and the course taken by men who rely on Nature and reason is this: the natural man travels on a straight line because it is the shortest, whereas religion travels in a circle. In religion, man rejects himself only to posit himself again in a glorified form; and he rejects his life here and now, but only to posit it again in the end as the life hereafter.

Religion thus arrives, though by a circuit, at the very goal toward which the natural man hastens in a straight line.

To live in projected dream-images is the essence of religion. Religion sacrifices reality to the projected dream: the "Beyond" is merely the "Here" reflected in the mirror of imagination.

Our essential task is now fulfilled. We have reduced the other-wordly, supernatural, and superhuman nature of God to the elements of human nature. We have arrived in the end to where we started from in the beginning. The beginning, the center, and the final goal of religion is—Man.

PART TWO

The False or Theological Essence
of Religion

CHAPTER XIII

The Contradiction in the Existence of God

When theology, by philosophical arguments, attributes a real, but unverifiable existence to God, the contradiction involved leads to atheism.

Religion is the relation of man to his own nature—therein lies its truth and its power of moral amelioration; but to man's nature not recognized as his own, but regarded as a distinct being, different from, or even opposed to, man—therein lies its untruth, its limitation, its contradiction to reason and morality.

To make of human nature a distinct, separately existing being is, however, in the original conception of religion an involuntary, childlike, simple act of the mind, that is, one which separates God and man just as rashly as it again identifies them. But when religion advances in years, and, with years, in understanding; when, within the bosom of religion, reflection on religion is awakened, and the consciousness of the identity of the divine nature with human nature begins to dawn—in a word, when religion becomes theology, then the originally involuntary and harmless separation of God from man becomes an intentional, excogitated distinction, which has no other aim than to banish again from our consciousness this identity of which we have become already aware.

Hence the nearer religion stands to its beginning, the truer, the more genuine it is, the less is its true nature disguised. That is to say, in the earliest stages of religion there is no qualitative or essential distinction whatever between God and man. And the religious man is not shocked at this identification, for his understanding is still in harmony with his religion. Thus in ancient Judaism, Jehovah was a being differing from the human individual in nothing but in duration of existence; in his qualities, his inherent nature, he was entirely like man—had the same passions, the same human, nay, even corporeal properties.

The first method used by theology to make the divine nature a distinct being and to place it outside of man, is to make the existence of God the object of a formal proof.

The proofs of the existence of God have been pronounced contradictory to the essential nature of religion. They are! But only in their form as proofs. Religion represents the inner nature of man naively and without reflection as an objective, distinct being. And the proof aims at nothing more than to prove that religion is right: the most perfect being is that than which no higher can be conceived: God is the highest that man conceives or can conceive. This premise of the ontological proof—the most interesting proof, because it proceeds from within—expresses the inmost nature of religion. That which is the highest for man, that from which he cannot turn away, that is to him God—*id quo nihil majus cogitari potest*. But this highest being would not be the highest if it did not exist; we could then conceive a higher being who would be superior by the addition of existence. But not to exist is a deficiency; to exist is perfection, happiness, bliss. From a being to whom man gives all, offers up all that is precious to him, he cannot withhold the bliss of existence. Contrary to religious feeling in the proof of the existence of God is only the fact that existence is thought of as something separate, which makes it appear that God is a mere conception, a being existing in the idea only—an appearance, however, which is immediately dissipated; for the very result of the proof is that to God belongs an existence distinct from a merely ideal one, an existence apart from man, apart from thought—a real self-existence.

The proof, therefore, is discordant with religious feeling only to the extent that it presents the implicit assumption of religion as a formal deduction, exhibits it in logical form,

THE CONTRADICTION IN THE EXISTENCE OF GOD

and therefore distinguishes what religion unites without analysis. For what is to religion the Highest, God, that it does not think as a mere abstract thought, but as something true and real. But that every religion does make an unconscious inference of this kind, is admitted in its polemic against other religions. "You heathens," says the Jew or the Christian, "were able to conceive nothing higher than your deities because you were sunk in sinful desires. Your God rests on a conclusion, the premises of which are your sensual impulses, your passions. You thought thus: the most excellent life is to live out one's impulses without restraint; and because this life was the most excellent, the truest, you made it your God. Your God was your carnal nature, your heaven only a free theater for the passions which, in society and under the conditions of actual life, had to suffer restraint." But, naturally, in relation to itself, no religion is conscious of such an inference.

The proofs of the existence of God attempt to change an internal ideal into something external, and to separate it from man. By his existence, God becomes an independent entity, a *Ding an sich:* he is not merely a being for us, a being in our faith, our feeling, our nature, he is also a being by himself, a being external to us—in a word, not merely a belief, a feeling, a thought, but also a real existent apart from belief, feeling, and thought. However, such an existence must necessarily be an existence accessible to our senses.

But God is not seen, not heard, not perceived by the senses. He does not exist for me, if I do not exist for him; if I do not believe in a God, there is no God for me. If I am not devoutly disposed, if I do not raise myself above the life of the senses, he has no place in my consciousness. Thus he exists only as long as he is felt, thought, believed in—the addition "for me" is unnecessary. His existence, therefore, is a real one; yet at the same time not a real one—it is a spiritual existence, says the theologian. But spiritual existence is only an existence in thought, in feeling, in belief, so that his existence is a medium between sensational existence and conceptional existence, a medium full of contradiction.

A necessary consequence of this contradiction is atheism. The existence of God is supposed to be an empirical existence, and yet it has none of the distinctive marks of an empirical existence. It calls upon man to seek it in the realm of reality; it impregnates his mind with sensational conceptions and expectations; hence, when these are not fulfilled, when, on the contrary, man finds that experience does not agree with these conceptions, he is perfectly justified in denying that existence.

CHAPTER XIV

The Contradiction in the Revelation of God

> *As long as "Revelation" is not seriously taken as something more than poetry, it can do no moral harm.*

With the idea of the existence of God is connected the idea of revelation. God's attestation of his existence, the authentic testimony that God exists, is revelation. Proofs drawn from reason are merely subjective; the objective, the only true proof of the existence of God is his revelation. A God who only exists without revealing himself, who exists for me only through my own mental act, such a God is a merely abstract, imaginary, subjective God; a God who gives me a knowledge of himself through his own act is alone a God who truly exists, who proves himself to exist, who is an objective God. Faith in revelation is the immediate certainty of the religious mind that what it believes, wishes, conceives, really is.

The belief in revelation exhibits in the clearest manner the characteristic illusion of the religious consciousness. The general premise of this belief is: man can of himself know nothing of God; all his knowledge is merely vain, earthly, human. Thus we know nothing of God beyond what he reveals to us. The knowledge imparted by God is alone divine, superhuman, supernatural knowledge. By means of revelation, therefore, we know God through himself; for revelation is the word of God—God declaring himself.

Nevertheless, divine revelation is determined by human nature. God speaks not to brutes or angels, but to men; hence he uses human speech and human conceptions. Man is an object to God before God perceptibly imparts himself to man; he thinks of man; he determines his own action in

57

accordance with the nature of man and his needs. God is, indeed, free in will; he can reveal himself or not; but he is not free in what he can think; he cannot reveal to man whatever he will, but only what is adapted to man, what is commensurate with human nature such as it actually is; he reveals what he must reveal, if his revelation is to be a revelation for man, and not for some other kind of being. Therefore, what God thinks for man is determined by the idea of man; it has arisen out of reflection on human nature. God puts himself in the place of man, and thinks of himself just as this other being can and should think of him; he thinks of himself not with his own thinking power, but with man's. In the scheme of his revelation God must have reference not to himself, but to man's power of comprehension. That which comes from God to man, comes to man only from Man-in-God, that is, only from the ideal nature of man to the phenomenal man, from the species to the individual.

Thus, there is merely an illusory distinction between divine revelation and so-called human reason or nature—the content of the divine revelation is of human origin, for it has proceeded not from God as God, but from God as determined by human reason and human wants. But this means: the content of revelation springs directly from human reason and human wants. And so, in revelation, man goes merely away from himself, in order to return, by a circuitous path, to himself! Here we have a striking confirmation of the assertion that the secret of theology is nothing else than anthropology.

Every revelation is simply a revelation of the nature of Man to existing men. Reason, the mind of the species, operates on the subjective, uncultured man only under the image of a personal being. Moral laws have force for him only as the commandments of a Divine Will which has at once the power to punish and the sight from which nothing escapes. That which man's own nature, his reason, his conscience tells him, does not bind him, because the subjective, uncultured man sees in conscience, in reason, in so far as he recognizes it as his own, no universal objective power; hence he must separate from himself that which gives him moral laws, must place it in opposition to himself as a distinct personal being.

Belief in revelation is a childlike belief, and is only respectable so long as it is childlike. But there is within us an inward necessity which impels us to present moral and philosophical doctrines in the form of narratives and fables, and an equal necessity to represent what we receive from within as a revelation from without. The mythical poet has an end in view—that of making men good and wise; he intentionally adopts the form of fable as the most appropriate and vivid method of representation; but at the same time, he is himself driven to this mode of teaching by his love of fable, by his inward impulse. So it is with a revelation enunciated by an individual. This individual has an aim; but at the same time he himself lives in and with the very ideas by means of which he realizes this aim. Man, by means of his imagination, involuntarily objectifies his inner nature and represents it as existing outside of himself. This objectified nature of the species is God.

> *By changing the results of human moral insight into God-made laws, the belief in revelation produces external, not internal conformity to morality.*

But just as Nature unconsciously produces results which look as if they were produced consciously, so revelation generates moral actions which do not, however, proceed from morality: it produces moral actions, but no moral dispositions. Moral rules are indeed observed, but they are severed from the inward disposition, the heart, by being represented as the commandments of an external law-giver, by being placed in the category of arbitrary laws, of police regulations. What is done is done not because it is good and right, but because it is commanded by God. The inherent quality of the deed is indifferent; and whatever God commands is right.

CHAPTER XV

The Contradiction of Faith and Love

In spite of Christianity's insistence that God is love, the restriction of love by faith has catastrophic results.

At first sight, faith appears to be only an unprejudiced separation of believers from unbelievers. But this separation is a highly critical distinction. The believer has God for him; the unbeliever against him. It is only as a possible believer that the unbeliever has God not against him—and therein precisely lies the ground of the demand that he should leave the ranks of unbelief. But that which has God against it is itself against God. To believe, is synonymous with goodness; not to believe, with wickedness. Faith, narrow and prejudiced, explains all unbelief by assuming that it is intentional. In its view, the unbeliever is an enemy to Christ out of obduracy, out of wickedness. Hence faith has fellowship with believers only; unbelievers it rejects. For what God rejects, man must not accept or tolerate; that would be a criticism of the divine judgment.

To love the man who does not believe in Christ, is a sin against Christ, is to love the enemy of Christ. That which God, which Christ does not love, man must not love either; such a love would be opposition to the divine will, consequently a sin. God, it is true, loves all men; but only when and because they are Christians, or at least only because they can be or want to be Christians. To be a Christian is to be beloved by God; not to be a Christian is to be hated by God, is to be an object of divine anger. The Christian must therefore love only Christians, others he must love only as possible Christians. The maxim, "Love your enemies," has reference only to personal enemies, not to public enemies, not to the enemies of God, to the enemies of faith, to unbelievers. If I love the men who deny Christ, who do not believe Christ, I betray and deny my Lord and God. Faith abolishes the natural ties of humanity; it replaces universal, natural unity by partisan unity.

Thus faith is essentially a spirit of partisanship. He who is not for Christ is against him. Faith knows only friends or enemies, it understands no neutrality; it is preoccupied only with itself. Faith is essentially intolerant; essentially, because with faith is always associated the illusion that its cause is the cause of God, its honor His honor. Tolerance on the part of faith would be intolerance towards God, who has the right to unconditional, undivided sovereignty. Nothing shall subsist, nothing exist, which does not acknowledge God, which does not acknowledge faith: "That at the name of Jesus every knee should bow, of things in heaven and things on earth, and things under the earth; and that every tongue should confess that Jesus Christ is Lord, to the glory of the Father." Therefore faith postulates a future world where faith has no longer an opposite, or where at least this opposite exists only in order to enhance the self-complacency of triumphant faith. Hell sweetens the joys of happy believers. "The elect will come forth to behold the torments of the ungodly, and at this spectacle they will not be smitten with sorrow; on the contrary, while they see the unspeakable sufferings of the ungodly, they, intoxicated with joy, will thank God for their own salvation." (Peter Lombard)

Faith is the opposite of love. Faith necessarily passes into hatred, hatred into persecution, wherever the power of faith meets with no opposition, wherever it does not find itself in collision with a power foreign to faith, with the power of love, of humanity, of the sense of justice. Faith left to itself necessarily feels itself superior to the laws of natural morality. The doctrine of faith is the doctrine of duty towards God—the highest duty towards God is faith. By how much God is higher than man, by so much higher are duties to God than duties toward man; and duties toward God necessarily come into collision with common human duties. For God is not only believed in, and conceived of, as a generic being dwelling alike in all men. Such faith would be the faith of love. He is also conceived of as a personal being, as a being by himself. To the extent, therefore, that God becomes a distinct being separated from human nature, to that extent are duties to God separated from duties to man: faith is, in religious sentiment, separated from morality, from love.

God is love. This is the sublimest dictum of Christianity. But the contradiction of faith and love is contained in this very proposition. Love is only a predicate, God the subject. What, then, is this subject in distinction from love?

I must necessarily ask this question and make this distinction. The necessity of the distinction would be done away with only if it were said conversely: Love is God, love is absolute existence. In the proposition "God is Love," it is not love which alone fills my soul: I leave a place open for my uncharitableness by thinking of God as a subject in distinction from the predicate. It is therefore inevitable that at one moment I lose the thought of love, at another the thought of God, that at one moment I sacrifice the personality of God to the divinity of love, at another the divinity of love to the personality of God.

This theoretic contradiction must necessarily manifest itself practically. Necessarily: for in Christianity love is tainted by faith, it is not free, it is not apprehended truly. A love which is limited by faith is an untrue love. Love knows no law but itself; it is divine through itself; it needs not the sanction of faith; it is its own justification. The love which is bound by faith is a narrow-hearted, false love, contradicting the idea of love, i.e., self-contradictory. It is a love which has only a semblance of holiness, for it hides in itself the hatred that belongs to faith; it is only benevolent so long as faith is not injured.

Christian love is a particular love, limited by the very epithet "Christian." But love is in its nature universal. So long as Christian love does not renounce its qualification of Christian, does not make love, simply, its highest law, so long is it a love which by its particularity is in contradiction with the nature of love, an abnormal, loveless love, which has therefore long been justly an object of sarcasm.

Man is to be loved for man's sake. Man is an object of love because he is an end in himself, because he is a rational and loving being. This is the moral law of the species, the law of intelligence. This love should be immediate, and only if it is immediate, directed directly at my fellowman, is it love. But if I, who can realize and fulfill my human nature only through love, interpose between my fellow man and myself the idea of an individual in whom the ideal of the species is supposed to be already realized, I annihilate the very essence of love and disturb the unity between me and my fellow man by the idea of a third person external to us. My fellow man is then an object of love to me only on account of his resemblance or relation to this model, not for his own sake, not on account of his nature.

Christ is nothing but a symbol, under which the unity of the species has impressed itself on the popular consciousness. Christ loved men: he wished to bless and unite them all without distinction of sex, age, rank, or nationality. Christ is the love of mankind to itself embodied in a symbol or in a person—but in a person who as a religious object has only the significance of a symbol, of an ideal.

He, therefore, who loves man for the sake of man, who rises to the love of the species, to that universal love which alone is adequate to the nature of the species, he is a Christian, is Christ himself. He does what Christ did, what made Christ Christ. Thus, where there arises the consciousness of the species as a species, the idea of humanity as a whole, Christ disappears. His true nature, however, does not disappear; for he was the substitute for the consciousness of the species, he was the symbol through which humanity taught the people that the consciousness of the species should be the law governing their lives.

CHAPTER XVI

A Practical Conclusion

My relation to religion is no merely negative relation. It is a critical relation. I only separate the true from the false, though it cannot be denied that the truth thus separated from falsehood is always a new truth, essentially different from the old.

Religion is the first form of the self-consciousness of man. Holy, therefore, are all religions, for they have saved for posterity this first form of consciousness.

But that which in religion ranks first—namely, God—is, as I have shown, in truth and in reality something second; for God is merely the projected essence of Man.

What, therefore, ranks second in religion—namely, Man—that must be proclaimed the first and recognized as the first.

If the nature of Man is man's Highest Being, if to be human is his highest existence, then man's love for Man must in practice become the first and highest law. *Homo homini Deus est*—man's God is MAN. This is the highest law of ethics. THIS IS THE TURNING POINT OF WORLD HISTORY.